I WAS ONCE A KID, TOO!

by H. R. Lederfeind

illustrated by
C. Gershbaum

ISBN-13: 978-1-56871-672-5

Published by:
TARGUM PUBLISHERS
editor@targumpublishers.com

In Conjunction with:
Ktav Publishers & Distributors Inc.
527 Empire Blvd. | Brooklyn, NY 11225
Tel: 718-972-5449 | Fax: 718-972-6307
orders@ktav.com

Originally published by Jewish Children's Book Club
105 Grove Street, Monsey NY 10952
BookClub613@gmail.com
in conjunction with Torah Umesorah
The National Society for Hebrew Day Schools

Dear Parents (and Grandparents).

We had a lot of fun writing and illustrating this book. The topic of the old fashioned simple fun that use to be the norm sparked many fond memories and conversations in our families. It was a nice opportunity for us to convey what it was like in the "good old days." Some things stayed the same and some are very different! We hope this book will be used as a spring board for fun and bonding conversations with your children and grandchildren.

We would like to dedicate this book to our amazing children. may they always be a source of inspiration and nachas to us. We would also like to dedicate this book to the memories of summer and simple fun at the old Mintz and Highland Park Bungalow colonies of the 1980's and 90's.

H.R.L and C.G.

Acknowledgement

I would like to acknowledge my family, my husband R' Eliezer Lederfeind and my children, Menachem Mendel, Moshe Don, Chaim Ozer, Gittel Rochel , Leiby and Toby. Much of this book is a result of the creativity and productivity of their youth. I am proud to share it with others. We thank Hashem for the wonderful people our children have grown up to be and wish them continued Hatzlacha and Bracha from Shamayim in all that they do.

Henna Rivka Lederfeind

"Abba, I'm bored.
There is nothing to do.
My batteries are dead
And I'm feeling quite blue.

"Abba, please tell me –
What did you do
When you were my age,
Were you once a kid, too?"

Abba smiled and slid his yarmulke
Over his eyes.
He put up his feet
And gave one of his sighs.

"You think that I'm old?!
I am just thirty-two!
That really is not so much
Older than you.

"Whatever the season,
Whatever the weather,
My good friends and I
Had simple fun all together.

Photos

Fall

CAN YOU FIND:

The old fashioned roller skates?

The Tinker Toys?

The squirrel riding a scooter?

"On cool, crisp Fall days
We did not stay inside
We ran out to play.
We had bikes to ride.

3
Rider

"Up and down the block
Us little kids would go.
Sometimes we'd be brave -
Pick up our hands to "Let Go!"

"We raked leaves in a pile
And ran to jump in,

Found acorns and pinecones,
Flew kites in the wind.

"And if skies were grey
And rain clouds would shower,
We would play inside
For hour after hour.

"Checkers and chess
Card games, too.
Monopoly and Scrabble
There was so much to do.

Winter

CAN YOU FIND:

Old fashioned ear muffs?

A hearing aid?

A red mitten?

The Aleph Bais in two places?

"The cold winter days meant
Snowmen and snowballs.
We shoveled and shoveled.
We never went to malls.

"We made a snow fort
For a big snowball fight.
And then we built igloos
And crawled in, out of sight.

"And just like a little boy
That I know
My mother would treat us
To cookies and hot cocoa!

"We would also learn Torah.
Yes, that is true.
Especially if we said
We had nothing to do.

"We would learn for a while
And then get a treat.
Learning and noshing
Just couldn't be beat.

Spring

CAN YOU FIND:

The girl hiding in a tree?

The hedgehog?

Birds in a nest?

A cassette tape?

"When the blossoms bloomed
And the weather was fair,
We'd run, jump and play
In the fresh Spring air.

"We played cops and robbers;
We played capture the flag;
We played hide and seek;
We played games of freeze tag.

"We used our imaginations
To build an easel and chair.
So what if they wobbled?
We kids didn't care!

"We made a basketball hoop
From an old milk crate.
The ball went in - but not out -
It wasn't that great.

"We would work
to keep busy
We had a grand plan.
Each week
we would wash
The family van.

"I weeded the garden
And planted some flowers;
I even made money!
A whole thirteen dollars!

Summer

CAN YOU FIND:

A strip of fly paper?

A tire swing?

A slice of watermelon?

A bird drinking lemonade?

"On long Summer days
We did not go to school.
We had lots of free time
And we tried to keep cool.

lemonade
5¢

"We ran through the sprinkler;
We sold cold lemonade.
With our neighbors and friends,
We relaxed in the shade.

"In the old bungalow colony
We played in the swamp.
On the freshly washed floors
All the mud we would stomp!

"We caught salamanders
We searched high and low.
We chased after fireflies
And captured their glow.

"We were acrobats in a circus!
We made a human pyramid.
We did tumbles and twirls
And included every kid.

28
29
18

"We swam in the pool;
We ran relay races;

We played 'Steal the Salami,'
We painted our faces!

"Sometimes we got in trouble
Our mothers were upset;
But they knew in their hearts
That we'd grow up yet."

"Yes, now I grew up,
And I do grown up things.
But I always kept skills
That old-fashioned play brings:

"Playing builds healthy bodies;
Playing helps you grow strong;
Playing helps you make friends;
You will always belong."

Abba leaned forward and smiled
And gave one of his sighs
He put down his feet
And looked me in the eyes.

Photos

Then suddenly Abba
Gave a BIG JUMP.
He said, "Tag! You're it!"
And gave my back a soft thump!

We ran through the house,
And then out the door!
Up and down the block
Three times or more!

Then all of our neighbors
Opened their doors wide
To see what was causing
The commotion outside.

And out from those doors
Kids and fathers flew!
Running and laughing –
Fathers once WERE kids, too!

We were laughing and running
And tagging so fast
All the fathers and children
Simply had a blast!

We plopped down on the grass
with a huff and a puff.
We looked around and said
"Hey, we like this stuff!

We like to play,
We like to run.
We like to have
Simple fun!"

Now when my batteries are dead,
Abba's words come to mind.

Whatever the season,
Simple fun I can find.

Bye!
Have Fun!